BLUFF YOUR WAY
IN
PARIS

JIM HANKINSON

ꆰ

Ravette London

Published by Ravette Limited
3 Glenside Estate, Star Road,
Partridge Green, Horsham,
Sussex RH13 8RA
(0403) 710392

Series Editor – Anne Tauté

Cover design – Jim Wire
Typesetting – Input Typesetting Ltd.
Printing & Binding – Cox & Wyman Ltd.
Production – Oval Projects Ltd.

The Bluffer's Guides are based on an
original idea by Peter Wolfe.

CONTENTS

Areas	11	Literature	43
		Living	22
Banlieue, La	19		
Bars	27	Marais	14
Beaux Arts	36	Montmartre	17
Belleville	19	Montparnasse	16
		Music	42
Cinema	40		
Clubs	30	Police	33
		Politics	44
Doctors	36	Props	10
Eiffel	17	Restaurants	22
Getting Around	7	Sex	30
Glossary	56	Seizième, Le	14
		St. Germain des Prés	16
History of Paris	46		
Latin Quarter	13	Theatre	40
Lavatories	34	Transport	7

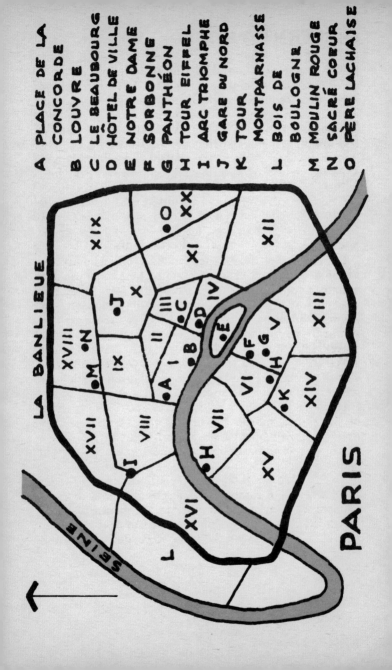

PARIS

LA BANLIEUE

SEINE

A PLACE DE LA
   CONCORDE
B LOUVRE
C LE BEAUBOURG
D HÔTEL DE VILLE
E NOTRE DAME
F SORBONNE
G PANTHÉON
H TOUR EIFFEL
I ARC TRIOMPHE
J GARE DU NORD
K TOUR
   MONTPARNASSE
L BOIS DE
   BOULOGNE
M MOULIN ROUGE
N SACRÉ COEUR
O PÈRE LACHAISE

INTRODUCTION

Paris: the very name is rich in an indelible array of unforgettable associations; the city that exercises an irresistible seductive appeal, from the lyrics of countless popular ballads, to the purple prose of holiday brochures, poets and artists have sung the praises of this incomparable, bewitching, enchanting city. The restaurants and bars of the Latin Quarter; the steep, winding streets of Montmartre; the formal grandeur of the Tuileries; the baroque magnificence of the Place des Vosges; the elegance of the great boulevards of the Second Empire; the raffish charm of its several red-light districts, which cater for all tastes at surprisingly low prices.

Paris is one of those places that anyone who aspires to make any kind of impact in the smart, upwardly-mobile, young-professional, successful world that one reads about in the Sunday newspapers simply has to know about. And if, like the rest of us, you aren't as upwardly mobile as you'd like to be, this book is the perfect solution. A week-end in Paris, after you've taken in a bit of culture, eaten at a few restaurants, sipped a **citron pressé** at a number of cafés, and generally indulged yourself in an appropriately sybaritic way, will set you back at least £200. For a fraction of the price, this book will tell you all you need to know in order to give the impression that you have done so, an impression invaluable in the right company.

The Golden Rule for the Paris bluffer is to use as much French in conversation as possible, and to make it as incomprehensible as possible: the glossary should be an invaluable guide here, but careful attention to the rest of the book will be rewarded. It is also

5

important when dealing with Paris, which almost
everybody claims to have *some* knowledge of, to give
the impression that you have gone BEHIND the
familiar facade it presents to the uncurious tourist:
that you have penetrated to the real heart of **la vie
Parisienne** (not that any such thing actually exists of
course: but don't let on). You must feign close acquaintance with out-of-the-way quartiers in obscure parts of
the city, sing the praises of remote bars in dingy side-
streets, and claim to have discovered absurdly good
and inexpensive restaurants in improbable and inaccessible places. Remember: the more esoteric your
'information', the less chance there is of your being
rumbled.

And finally, it is important for all but the most brilliant, gifted and ambitious of bluffers to retain somewhere among the farrago of total balderdash and
misinformation that they will be disseminating, some
kernel of the truth: this is what gives the successful
charlatan his appearance of verisimilitude. That
(among other invaluable things) is what this book
supplies.

Note: And **when** should you be in Paris? There is only one
really clear answer to this question and that is 'Not in
August'. In August almost all of Paris decamps to the country
and the seaside, leaving behind a small residue of people
dedicated to fleecing tourists, and of course, the tourists
themselves. Spring, and early Summer are acceptable, but a
bit too touristique: September, if you can survive the insanity
of the **rentrée**, is all right too. March and October are
popular, and good value for that reason. But whichever you
choose the important thing is to convey the impression that
you have powerful but **recherché** reasons for going when
you do that mark you off from the common herd: it doesn't
much matter what they turn out to be.

GETTING AROUND

The younger Alexandre Dumas (who should be referred to as "Alexandre Dumas fils") remarked that 'God invented the Parisian to prevent foreigners from ever understanding anything about the French.' And all in all, he did a good job of it. You will never get a straight answer from a Parisian unless it happens to be a rude one: and even then you're unlikely to be much the wiser (although you might be a good deal sadder).

Transport

The first thing you will need to do is to master Paris public transport. The **Métro** is confusing. The rule is: don't buy a single ticket. Buy a **carnet** of ten tickets, which works out much cheaper. If you're in Paris for a month it makes sense to buy a monthly season, a **Carte Orange**, but you need a photo for that, and it's almost certainly not worth it unless you're there for the entire time. The Carte Orange varies in price according to which zones you want to use, but the city of Paris within the walls (see the next section), is all within zone 1, and in practice there is very little reason for going outside the walls (but note the section on **la Banlieue**).

The lines are numbered in the order in which they were constructed: thus the earliest line ran from Porte de Vincennes to Porte Maillot, and is now part of Ligne 1: but the Parisians never refer to the Métro by numbers, but rather by the names of the stations at the end of the lines. This makes for some confusion, as the Métro, unlike the London Underground, is still being added to. Early in 1985 what had been Place d'Italie-Eglise de Pantin became Place d'Italy-

Bobigny; but once you get used to it, it is surprisingly easy: the accomplished bluffer will express surprise that anyone finds any trouble with it at all, perhaps remarking, in a casual manner, that it's a good deal more comprehensible than the New York Subway.

The Métro hardly extends beyond the walls (with the exception of the recent extensions), the legacy of a demarcation dispute of the last century between the Paris Urban Transport Authority (**RATP**) and French Railways (now **SNCF**). This dispute persists in the allocation of the new high-speed suburban underground system, the **RER** (which stands for **Reseau Electrique Régional**: you score points for remembering this), some of which is run by SNCF, some by RATP. This wouldn't matter much, except for the fact that Ligne B, which runs north-south and serves the airport at **Roissy** (never call it Charles de Gaulle) is divided in the middle. It means that, except at peak times you can't get a through train from the airport to the centre of the city, but have to change at the Gare du Nord. This is extremely irritating. Nonetheless, the RER is very quick and efficient, and has the great virtue that most tourists don't seem to use it, perhaps unaware that, within the walls at least, their ordinary Métro tickets are valid on it.

It is important to know that, both on the ordinary Métro and on the RER, you have to open the doors yourself, either by raising a handle (on the older carriages), or by pressing a button (on the newer ones, and on the RER). If you fail to do so, you run the risk of being carried on to a place you did not want to go. The seasoned Paris hand raises the handle slightly before the train stops in order to open the door at the earliest possible opportunity, thus giving the impression both of businesslike haste (only tourists hang around waiting for things to happen) and an easy familiarity with the workings of the city.

As for the **autobus**, though each bus-stop has a diagram of the route posted on it, it is difficult to put the marks on these diagrams into any kind of correspondence with any other representation of the city. It is best, if you use them at all, simply to go to the places on the direction boards, or to go with people who know what they're doing. Asking the bus-drivers results in blank stares (not shrugs: the French, contrary to popular belief, hardly ever shrug, and they don't gesticulate that much either), unless your French is perfect: and if your French *is* perfect, you're unlikely to have to ask in the first place, a peculiarly Gallic form of Catch–22.

And that leaves **taxis**. It is very important to realise that, although Paris taxis look like private cars with meters inside and lights on the roof, no passenger is allowed in the front passenger seat.

The best way to see things is on foot; but this has to be done surreptitiously if you want to avoid giving the impression of being a tourist. It is a good idea to try and walk as fast as the nearest suited executive. This will take you past the great monuments and public buildings at a brisk rate of knots – but you might just be able to catch sight of them out of the corner of your eye. Pedestrian crossings are painted on the roads in a spirit of forlorn hope, and any driver who takes notice of them is regarded by his fellows as a cissy. What you have to do is walk nonchalantly out into the traffic with your move timed in such a way as to avoid most of the oncoming vehicles, and to force the rest of them to swerve violently. This is not as easy as it sounds, and requires a great deal of practice. It is important to remember that the genuine Parisian does not quicken his pace while crossing roads: if anything he goes more slowly.

Props

In Paris you must have a view about which newspaper to read. This is partly a matter of politics, partly a matter of tone. No-one who wants to be taken seriously in matters of style would read the Communist *Humanité*, for instance. *Le Monde*, which is mildly left-wing, is a possibility, but it is rather serious and heavy going (this is true even of the regular humorous column on the back page). For the young, smart, fashionably cynical socialist, the essential reading is *Libération*, a well-written, irreverent left-wing daily, known familiarly as **Libé**. If you're trying to project a New Right image, and a lot of people are these days, then *Figaro* is the one to get.

As for magazines, *never* be seen with *Paris Match*. For women, *Elle* and *Marie Claire* are acceptable. Men are advised to steer clear of them altogether, but might try reading ostentatiously a copy of *Hari-Kiri* (an unrelievedly obscene, and occasionally very funny satirical magazine).

Lifestyle in Paris is often largely a matter of where you live and what you do for a living. If you live in the **Banlieue**, wear leather jackets, drive a motorbike and are on the dole, then you are a **loubard** (good-for-nothing). If, on the other hand, you live in the Seizième, wear designer clothes, drive an Alfa Romeo, and are not on the dole, you are **BCBG** (pronounced 'baysay-bayjay'). This is an extremely important social classification, standing for **bon chic, bon genre**, a concept with no direct equivalent in English, but which connotes wealth, style, and a certain social **savoir-faire**. It has some, but by no means all, the connotations of 'Sloane Ranger' in English. It is vital for the bluffer to develop a confidence in the use of these terms.

Areas

Paris is a compact city, and it's compactness is enhanced by the fact that there is not all that much outside the centre that you really need to know about.

Paris is divided formally into twenty **arrondissements**, informally into innumerable **quartiers**. An **arrondissement** is roughly equivalent to a London borough, each having its own **Mairie** (small town hall). **Quartier** has no English equivalent, although it is similar to the American 'neighbourhood'. Always refer to both in French, of course.

The Parisians very rarely use the word 'arrondissement' themselves, but refer instead cryptically to 'the Sixteenth' or 'the Fifth', as indeed should you. The **arrondissements** are arranged in a spiral starting from the centre of Paris and working out to the edges rather like a snail ('comme un escargot', of course). **Le Premier**, then, is right in the heart of the city.

Le Premier

It contains **Chatelet** and **Hôtel de Ville**, two major meeting places in town. Hôtel de Ville has been cleaned up and turned into a pedestrian area, a large windswept field of paving stones. Chatelet, with its pleasant central column and fountain (if you can negotiate the traffic to get to it) hasn't. The **Ile de la Cité**, where **Notre Dame** is situated, is also in the Premier: the square in front of the cathedral is always full of Scandinavian tourists and their backpacks, and is definitely not a place to be seen.

Of the islands in the Seine, infinitely perferable is the smaller and quieter **Ile St. Louis**. It is traversed from end to end by the picturesque rue de St. Louis-en-l'Ile which is bounded by beautiful, quiet old **hôtels**. (Be warned: in this sense hôtel does not mean 'hotel' – it rather refers to large 17th and 18th century buildings that surround a courtyard. Most of them are still private apartments, where you can still buy a nice little place of four or five rooms or so for less than a million pounds – if you're lucky.) The other crowning glory of the Ile St. Louis is that it contains at least five shops selling the magnificent **Berthillon** ice-cream (don't forget to say you've eaten one: invent a suitable exotic flavour).

On the other side of the Premier, on the Right Bank (**rive droite**, of course) is the extraordinary modern complex of **Les Halles**. Note: it is very important to pronounce this as two separate words, 'Lay Al', not, as the English showing off their atrocious French are liable to do, as one word with liaison, 'layzal'. This was the central food market of Paris, the Covent Garden, Billingsgate and Smithfield rolled into one, but larger, as it controlled food distribution for much of France. In the old days housewives would come here in the early morning to get fresh food for the day. But in the sixties the planners decided it couldn't stay where it was (the traffic problems were appalling), and the whole thing was moved out to a new site at **Rungis** in the suburbs, where housewives don't go in the early morning to get fresh food for the day.

Apart from the central area, you need to know about the following areas within the walls:

The Latin Quarter

On the Left Bank (**rive gauche**) opposite Notre Dame is the famous **quartier Latin**, former haunt of writers, artists and musicians and large numbers of people pretending to be writers, artists and musicians. Now it only contains the latter group, it is fashionable to denigrate the area as a mere tourist attraction (which is a pity). The most attractive part is the montagne St. Geneviève up near the **Panthéon**, a huge neo-classical architectural blot which contains the bodies of famous dead Frenchman, as well as lots of bodies of dead Frenchman wrongly considered by the French to be famous. The inscription over the door, *Aux Grands Hommes d'une Patrie Reconaissante* (to great men from a grateful fatherland) manages uniquely to combine a grotesque sexism with a peculiarly unpleasant type of nationalistic patriotism. Here lie the remains of large numbers of Presidents and great men (Victor Hugo, Voltaire, Rousseau, Emile Zola, Louis Braille) and just one woman (Madame Berthelot).

The centre of this area is the Place Contrescarpe, and the **rue Mouffetard** which runs through it contains some of the pleasantest and more inexpensive restaurants in Paris. Here too, is the major university of Paris, and one of the oldest in Europe, **La Sorbonne**. Once the centre of the student revolt of May 1968 still referred to neutrally by the French as **Les événements** (the events), nowadays the place has a fairly right-wing reputation. The centre of the university is, appropriately enough, the Place de la

Sorbonne, a small pedestrian square off the Boulevard St. Michel (which should *always* be referred to as the **Boul'Mich**), and, during the terms at least, full of students looking exceptionally **cool**. Scruffiness is not admired these days, if indeed it ever was in Paris.

The Marais

The crowing glory of the **Quatrième** is the **Marais**, the old Jewish quartier of Paris (which still houses a sizeable Jewish population, particularly around the **rue des Rosiers**). This is one of the oldest parts of town, fallen into disrepair by the end of the war, but now entirely restored to its former beauty and value. To live in a flat in one of the **hôtels** looking onto such a courtyard is the dream of the young **snobiste**.

The **Place des Vosges**, is a perfectly preserved, colonnaded seventeenth-century square, with a green space in the centre, also surprisingly free from tourists. The whole area is alive with small restaurants, clubs, bars, delicatessens, and kosher butchers, some of whom suffered in the wave of anti-semitic violence in the early eighties, conducted by nastier members of the Nouvelle Droite, the best known target being the famous Jewish restaurant, **Goldenberg's**.

Le Seizième

This is just across the river from the drab and undistinguished Quinzième, but it might be a whole world away. And indeed its inhabitants behave as though it is. The **Seizième** is more than just an **arrondissement**: it's a complete package of **haute-**

bourgoise, expensive life-style. If you say of someone that they're **"seizième"**, you mean more than that's where they live. You mean, among other things, that they are extremely well off, went to extremely good schools (often public **lycées**) and, if they are women, probably to finishing schools as well. They are as well-dressed as they are well-heeled, they drive a turbo-charged Renault in town and a Mercedes out of it, probably have a country place in Provence or on the Côte d'Azur, perhaps own a yacht, belong to exclusive sports clubs, regularly take trips abroad, have several expensive mistresses if they're men, a fleet of hunky gigolos if they're women. In short, they live the life of gross, selfish, morally and politically unacceptable capitalism, the lucky bastards. They are BCBG in a big way.

All of the Seizième is classy, but that part of it which backs onto the Bois de Boulogne, from the **Porte d'Auteuil** up to the **Avenue Foch**, is probably the most exclusive and expensive part of the quartier, and consequently the one you're least likely to get invited to. People there live in large, architect-designed apartments generally filled with original works of art and the obligatory hideous Louis Quinze reproduction furniture – except that some of it may be genuine hideous Louis Quinze furniture. Like everything else in Paris, however, gross ostentation is done with style. You can't faze these people. The proper form of Seizième behaviour is to affect a kind of frigid politeness that serves to reveal rather than to conceal an almost infinite depth of boredom and contempt for the rest of the world. Politics are invariably world-weary right-wing. Cynicism is perhaps the best available line, but you've got to carry it through with style: they're almost certainly better at it than you are.

St. Germain des Prés

St. Germain des Prés boasts a charming church and two famous cafés, the **Deux Magots** and the **Café de la Flore**. These large and outrageously expensive emporia stand side-by-side at St. Germain, and they used at least to be the haunt of writers and journalists, and the generally arty (e.g. **Jean-Paul Sartre**). Nowadays they are patronised principally by people hoping to see a writer, a journalist or someone generally arty. There is no harm in pretending that you have identified (or better still, talked to) one of these people there (you could try **Alain Robbe-Grillet**, or **Philippe Sollers**, or if really confident, invent a young, and as-yet-unheard-of literary lion).

At all events, anyone who actually knows these places will be impressed that you've even managed to afford a cup of coffee there let alone spotted a celebrity; and they are good places to be seen in. Paris, like anywhere else these days, demands being seen in and you could try and get yourself casually filmed in any one of the dozens of pop videos that seem to be being made around the cafés all the time.

Montparnasse

Montparnasse is a name of some resonance, despite its 'redevelopment', the **pièce de résistance** of which is the gross and unimaginative **Tour Montparnasse**, six hundred feet of phallic ugliness stuck on top of the rebuilt concrete railway station. Here and there old streets remain, such as the **rue Raymond Losserand**. It is still just about possible, if armed with a clandestine bottle of Absinthe and a blindfold, to recreate the Bohemian atmosphere of the twenties, when Montparnasse was the chief haunt of expatriate British and American writers and artists (at least the more successful ones: people like **Henry Miller** had to live in unfashionable Clichy). It is worth knowing that such luminaries as **Jean Rhys**, **Ford Madox Ford**, **Gertrude Stein** and **Ernest Hemingway** all lived and slept with each other around here just after the First World War.

Eiffel

No comment on Paris would be complete without saying something about the **Eiffel Tower**. Erected in 1889 for no very obvious reason, except that there was a Paris Exhibition at the time, and it was big, the Eiffel Tower was to have been demolished immediately afterwards. Many wish that it had been. As powerful and misleading a symbol of all things French as accordion music and men in stripy T-shirts, the Eiffel Tower has dominated the Paris skyline with its gross cast-iron bulk ever since. On no account go up it, don't even *think* of doing so. This is the most important rule of all for the bluffer in Paris: THE EIFFEL TOWER MUST BE DESPISED.

Montmartre

Montmartre is principally associated in most tourists' minds with the large white excrescence of **Sacré Coeur** (not to be confused with "sacré bleu!", an archaic French expletive), in celebration of the bloody repression of the Paris commune (see History). It is built on secure foundations, unfortunately, that stretch right through the hill (**la Butte de Montmartre**) it rests on. It is, along with the Eiffel Tower and the Tour Montparnasse, one of the three most visible landmarks of Paris, and from a distance it resembles a large, vulgar wedding-cake. The prudent will avoid this place at all costs, and regularly say so.

But this is not the real Montmartre. The real Montmartre, the bluffer never tires of pointing out, the centre of literary and artistic activity in the city towards the end of the last century, and still beautiful and relatively quiet, is located to the south-west of the Place du Tertre. Steep winding streets connected by flights of stone steps, small, inexpensive restaurants, including one of Paris's better-known vegetarian places on the rue des Trois Frères, called, wittily, **Au Grain de Folie***, little bars run by decrepit old couples, decaying hotels with paper-thin walls through which one can hear the activities of discerning couples on dirty week-ends or **weekend amoureux** as the French more poetically call it: this is the real Montmartre. It is most easily approached up the hill from the Métro at Abbesses, if you can fight your way past an impressive convention of tramps who regularly congregate there. It is best seen in the late afternoon and early evening, when the hillside faces the sinking sun. To walk, on an evening in early summer, up one of the narrow streets past a wall covered in blooming purple clematis: that is to have discovered the *real* Paris.

*A pun on **grain** (grain, in the sense of wheat, etc.), and the colloquial phrase "**Il a un grain de folie**": he's a bit dotty.

Belleville

It is important that the bluffer should make him or herself an 'expert' on one of the more out-of the-way and less prepossessing parts of the city. Ideal for this purpose is **Belleville**, on the borders of the **Onzième** and the **Dix-neuvième**, the shadowy world of corrupt police, gang warfare, drugs, protection rackets, pimping and shabby Algerian restaurants celebrated in **policiers** (see Cinema). But about the only one of these things you'd actually notice if you walk through it during the day is the preponderance of Algerian restaurants. In fact, it's quite easy to pass through the entire area without realising that you have.

On its flank, **Père Lachaise** contains the dead bodies of the French who are:

a) very nearly famous enough to make it to the Panthéon but not quite
b) fairly famous
c) downright insignificant.

It also contains the living bodies of numerous French homosexuals which you may stumble across (or over): indeed, the cemetary is now known by its habitués as '**Père Labaise**' (for a clue as to what this means, see Glossary under **baiser**).

La Banlieue

Outside the walls* lies the large, amorphous area known compendiously as **La Banlieue**: the suburbs. This is the bit you see most of coming in on the train, or on one of the main roads, and is best taken as quickly as possible. In fact, the habit of calling it by one dismissive and contemptuous name masks the fact that there is a considerable variety; and although no-one would claim that much of the Banlieue is actually pretty, certain bits of it have their supporters.

The Banlieue essentially comes in two basic sections. The nearer part, the **proche banlieue**, is the older bit, for many years drab, undistinguished, and extremely difficult to travel in as the Métro didn't extend into it as a result of the demarcation dispute. It thus acquired its persisting reputation of inconvenience and isolation, of generally being divorced from the real Paris: the **triste banlieue**. Beyond that inner ring of suburbs, a new outer ring has sprung up since the War, of vast new integrated housing developments. The first of these was at **Sarcelles** on the north side of the city, but this has been overshadowed by the **new towns**, the most striking of which is **Cergy-Pontoise** which when completed will be a large, self-contained town, with its own industry and leisure facilities, making it unnecessary to go into Paris at all.

The Banlieue is not fashionable: it would be a severe mistake to spend your only week-end in Paris holed up in Gennevilliers, Bobigny, or Créteil. But it isn't uniformly appalling: and it is good bluffing material as the casual visitor to Paris almost never goes anywhere near it, except on the way to and from the city. Recently there have been attempts to give the Banlieue a better image; posters have appeared in the Métro claiming that '**ça bouge, la banlieue**', roughly translated, 'the joint is really jumping out there' but

*Not that the walls now exist: their place is taken by the large orbital motorway, the **Boulevard Périphérique**: any association of leisure and lack of hustle conjured up by the word 'Boulevard' is entirely misleading.

no-one seems really to have been convinced. The Parisian attitude to the Banlieue is (as it is towards so many things) one of contempt, and people will happily pay three times as much in rent to avoid the terrible fate of being "**enterré dans la campagne**", literally "buried in the countryside". Anything outside the walls counts, for the purposes of this remark, more or less as the countryside. You should therefore claim to have discovered, somewhere not too inaccessible, a really pleasant **quartier** beyond the walls, preferably with a couple of good cheap restaurants, and a jazz club. You remark, in an off-hand way, how no-one who only knows Paris *within* the walls can really claim to know the city properly at all.

Every bluffer ought to have at least one 'favourite spot' outside: there are plenty to choose from:

- The Palace at **Versailles** – despite being well-known.
- **Fontainebleau** – because it's so far away.
- The old royal chapel at **St. Denis** – particularly as it is accessible by the Métro.
- Monet's house at **Giverny** – a good deal harder to get to, and for this reason alone, a best choice.

You could also become a partisan of one of the large open spaces outside the walls, the **Fôret de St. Germain**, perhaps, or the **Parc de St. Cloud**, to the west of the Bois de Boulogne. Or alternatively, simply adopt an area, such as **Romainville**, to the east of the walls, a quiet, pleasant district. Worth remembering in this regard is that, while Paris within the walls is a stronghold of the political Right (Jacques Chirac built his power-base as mayor of Paris: see Politics), the **Banlieue** is solidly Left. You might try claiming that this gives it a better atmosphere, or makes the people friendlier. As a matter of fact, it doesn't, but there's no harm in claiming so.

LIVING

For centuries, almost from time immemorial, Paris has been admired as the world's great capital of culture, Queen of Cities, the guardian of all that is most tasteful and stylish. Life for the Parisian is not simply a day-to-day matter of survival, or an undignified scramble for wealth and success: it is something to be lived as an art-form. It is impossible for even the briefest and most fleeting acquaintance with this most glorious of cities not to leave the traveller with a deep and abiding sense that here, of all the world's great capitals, civilisation has most nearly achieved its perfection.

So the bluffer must have a firm basis of more-or-less informed, powerfully-held views about the business of living in Paris if he or she is successfully to convey the impression of an easy, first-hand familiarity with the place.

Restaurants

Everyone thinks of food when they think of France, and it is still generally true that it is easier to find good food in Paris that it is in, say, Walsall. Nonetheless, the profile of the average Frenchman's eating habits (if not the profile of the average Frenchman) has changed considerably in recent years, and **le fast-food** has reared its ugly and indigestible head. Nor is it the case that the rash of hamburger joints which have sprung up accross the face of the city in recent years like a sort of gastronomic excema is entirely peopled by cultureless American tourists. There is a section of French youth who consider it **à la mode**

22

(remember: the French for chic, in the sense of 'fashionable', is not **chic**) to be seen chewing **un cheeseburger** in any one of the virtually indistinguishable chains. Wendy and Burger King have triumphed, although the unwary visitor might have been perplexed to discover that, until recently, there didn't seem to be any McDonald's outlets in Paris, and might have been equally puzzled by the existence of a chain rejoicing in the improbable, if surprisingly honest, name of O'Kitch. The solution to the enigma is simple: O'Kitch *is* McDonald's, or rather was, until the parent company withdrew its right to use the McDonald's name because their products failed to reach the requisite high standard. This astounding truth can provide you with a useful conversational line.

This trend towards Americanisation is a general one and should be deplored. Along with **le hamburger** there goes, inevitably, **le hot-dog**. The Parisians make no effort to Gallicise these names: The desperate attempts of the establishment to preserve the 'purity' of the French language are treated with total contempt by anyone with any street credibility (anyone, that is, who is **branché**, or better still, **chébran**: see Glossary).

If you have to have fast-food in Paris, much the best thing to do is go for North African. In any one of thousands of small Tunisian and Algerian cafés you can, with only a mild risk of salmonella, partake of a **sandwich tunisien**, a sort of tuna salad roll, or better still, a **sandwich merguez**. **Merguez** are viciously spicy, bright red Arab sausages, deposited in a foot long piece of French bread and covered with chips. In fact the proper name for this confection is **un sandwich-merguez-frites**, spoken at high speed as if it were one word. These can be quite delicious, although they vary enormously in quality from place to place. The good bluffer will have his or her favourite Tunisian café; the great thing about sandwich-merguez-frites is their inexpensiveness: for ten to twelve francs, you can get yourself a large, filling lunch.

In spite of all this, the traditional Paris café still exists. More popular at lunch-time than in the evening, and to be avoided unless outstandingly crowded, it is just about possible to get a perfectly good lunch for around forty francs. (This is still broadly true, and even if it isn't, it is important for you to *claim* that it is.) The rule with such places is never to divulge their identity or location, because of course once tourists get to hear about them they lose all their charm and get completely ruined. Hint darkly that you've found one in **the Marais**, or around Contrescarpe: or more adventurously, in some entirely unfashionable part of town, such as the **Treizième**, or even the **Banlieue**. The right type of place is recognisable by its air of frenetic activity, both on the part of the staff and the clientèle. The former are invariably harassed and overworked, except in the case of the barman, who generally seems to have time to stop and chat in a leisurely fashion with the customers apparently oblivious to the hell that is being let loose around him.

There are two ways of ascertaining what there is to eat (always go for the **menu**, which is not the French for 'menu' as you might expect, but means the set meal of the day). You can either attempt to read a chalk scrawl on a blackboard at the other side of the crowded room, or you can try decoding the unintelligible gabble of the waiter or waitress, a breed who think that efficiency demands that they speak at twice or three times the normal, already formidable, Paris velocity. It is absolutely vital that the Paris bluffer in Paris *never* give the impression of not having understood what has been said to them. To this end, some advice is in order.

It is useful to bear in mind that every **restau** (try calling them this) that does cheap lunches offers as an hors d'oeuvre **crudités**, bits of raw vagetable not to be confused with **charcuterie**, which is bits of dead pig, and **oeufs mayonnaise**: so you can't go wrong ordering those. As for the main course, if you say **steack** (French for steak), you're generally O.K., as it's a generic term covering a whole range of things like **faux-filet**, **contre-filet**, **entrecôte**, **pavé**, (literally, 'paving-stone' and figuratively, dirty great piece of meat), **bavette**, and many others. If asked what these various names correspond to in English, you will reply that of course the French don't butcher meat in the same way, so there are no real equivalents (this is very useful). As for vegetables, you're generally safe with **frites** – these days the French, like everyone else, seem to have chips with everything. They call it international **cuisine**. Similarly secure is **salade**: don't specify which sort, or if asked, gesticulate indeterminately and mumble 'salade de maison'. This usually works.

For desert, try cheese.

The French are inordinately interested in cheese, and will go to great lengths to ensure that the cheese they buy is just right. And they've got enough to choose from: General de Gaulle once remarked on the impossibility of uniting a nation that produced over two hundred and thirty varieties of cheese. Listen to a couple of Frenchmen arguing about cheese, and you will see what he meant. Restaurants always have Camembert. If they say they haven't got it, look disappointed, then accept the first thing offered in its stead.

This may of course turn out to be a monstrously odor-
iferous goat's cheese from the Auvergne, or a soap-
textured rubber-substitute from Alsace – but the
bluffer must suffer for his art. Just eat it, and don't
let on.

As for drink, you're safe with **vin de table du
Patron**, or **Cuvée du Patron**, or at least you're safe
ordering it. If it turns out to be like paint-stripper,
remark on its "sturdy peasant qualities of uncompro-
mising robustness". Don't forget to specify **blanc**,
rouge, or **rosé**. Many Parisians, however, don't drink
alcohol with their lunch, and you might cut a more
impressive figure ordering a mineral water. Always
specify a particular type, preferably not Perrier, which
is perfectly acceptable, but too well-known. Ideally,
you want to discover a little-known variety, then practise looking suitably distressed when they haven't got
it. Evian is quite a good bet, being slightly up-market.
If you want on the other hand to give the impression
of being **au fait** with the ordinary generalities of
French life, you could try Badoit.

If you do order a steak, you will be asked how you
want it cooked. This is not merely a polite formality,
with the final condition of the meat bearing no relation
whatever to your request. It is generally acted upon.
The important specifications are:

    seignant – rare (literally: bloody)
    à point – medium
    bien cuit – well-done and
    bleu – extremely rare.

The latter is the best (particularly so if you actually
do like your steaks rare), as it gives the impression of
acquaintance with the idiom. It should also be borne
in mind that the French, for whatever reason, seem to

imagine that the English prefer their meat reduced to the status of carbonised wreckage, so if they suspect you're English, they're likely to give you your meat more well-done than you want it. This belief contrasts interestingly with that of the Germans, for whom 'Englisch', when applied to meat at least, means 'rare'.

When you finish your meal, you will be offered coffee. A good move at this juncture is to decline, saying that you "know a good little bar just round the corner" where you can get really excellent **express**. You now signify to whoever is serving you that what in fact you want is the bill. The confident will demand not **l'addition**, but **la douloureuse**. That leaves the tip (even if you don't). In Paris almost all bars and restaus include service in the bill. If they don't, they're likely to go out of their way to make sure you're aware of the fact. But even if **service** is **compris**, it is still standard to leave a bit of loose change on the table.

Bars

Paris bars are in fact remarkably uniform places, falling basically into three categories.

1. There are the large, elegantly-mirrored **brasseries** that you find on the main boulevards and in the important squares, like the **Flore** and the **Deux Magots**. Inside, these consist of well-lit rooms with padded benches upholstered in red plastic round formica tables, and usually a fair number of potted plants; outside, of iron chairs covered in uncomfortable plastic cord round formica tables. They are staffed by a species of specially-cloned waiter, identically dressed in black trousers, dinner-jackets and bow-ties. The more ostentatious among them sport red waistcoats,

and sometimes even red bow ties. This is the nearest they go to individuality. They are very expensive indeed. Only use them for special reasons.

2. The second type resembles the first in its furnishings, but is smaller, generally darker and won't have as many mirrors. Instead, the walls are likely to be adorned with unspeakable prints of work by deservedly obscure artists, or, even worse, actual originals by deservedly obscure artists. They invariably (and this is a rule that applies to the third category as well) contain a huge dog,* more often than not an Alsatian, of terrifying strength and equally terrifying malevolence. These creatures tend to lurk under the tables ready to chew the feet of any customer rash enough to come within range. You have been warned. This sort of bar is much less expensive than the first, but is still liable to seem extortionate, particularly if you're drinking beer. In Paris the cheapest alcoholic drinks are wine (**un ballon de rouge** is an idiomatic way of ordering a large glass of red), and various types of Pernod-substitute lumped together as **pastis**. Unless you actually want a bottled beer, don't order **une bière**: the correct thing to ask for is **un demi**, literally 'a half', which by some bizarre process of Gallic logic, actually turns out to be a quarter of a litre of gassy draught lager of no discernable alcoholic content.

3. The third sort of bar is a down-market version of the second but dingier; usually a long, thin corridor

---

*They are one of the only two types of dog ever seen in Paris; the other is a type of hideously-spoiled and fantastically ugly lap-dog, much beloved of the **haute-bourgoise** ladies of the **Seizième**, and of the better class of prostitute (make sure you don't confuse these categories of female, as is surprisingly easily done).

stretching back from the street into a dimly illuminated nether darkness. Here dogs are even larger and shorter tempered, as indeed are the barmen.

As for the proper place to be in a bar, this is a matter of some dispute. It's always cheaper to stand at the bar than to sit at a table, and some bluffers prefer always to do this, believing it enhances their **branché** image. However, there are times when it is right to choose to sit, even to sit outside, particularly if the weather is nice. There are no real rules for this: it's something for your personal preference and judgement. The Parisians don't, generally, spend entire evenings in bars, as one might in a pub. Accordingly, it is not really **cool** to stay in the same place for much more than an hour or so. The best time to drop in for a quick drink is around six o'clock, as if you're just having a quick one on the way home from work. Nearly all bars, except for the really posh ones, have at least one pin-ball machine (though some are now being replaced with video-games), known as **le flipper**. On no account play the machine unless you are confident of doing extremely well.

Finally, it is proportionately much more expensive to drink in bars, as compared with buying the booze in a supermarket, in France than it is in Britain. While the bluffer must avoid looking like a cheapskate, it can be effective to suggest buying a bottle in one of the supermarkets, and drinking it in a park somewhere, along with some French bread. French bread, the long, thin variety, comes in three principal sizes, varying in gauge. The thickest is known simply as **pain**. Slightly thinner are **baguettes**; and thinnest of all are the **ficelles**. Best to go for baguettes. Having bought one, it is **de rigueur** to nibble absently at it as you walk away from the **boulangerie**.

Clubs

Unless you have some really good inside information avoid all Clubs in Paris. This is particularly true in the case of jazz clubs, which seem to change all the time. It is perhaps best to state firmly, if falsely, that real Parisians don't go to them in any case.

Sex

Paris has a reputation as a city of elegant sensuality, where sex and style go together to create a culture of studied, refined amorality; where the **spectacles érotiques** bear about as much resemblance to an East-end pub Sunday lunchtime strip-tease as **cordon-bleu** does to bubble and squeak. This is true, up to a point. But Paris's reputation as the place for acceptable naughtiness was made in the last century, and the rest of the world has done a lot of catching up. The classical symbols of Parisian decadent style, the **Moulin Rouge** and the **Folies Bergère** still exist (in the **Neuvième**, near Pigalle), but are unlikely to shock any but the most strait-laced – until, that is, they give you the bill.

It is no problem to find commercial erotic theatre of a more explicit nature – but it isn't really French, and is aimed much more at visitors. You should point this out. It does pay, however, to be aware of some of the sillier claims made for these establishments in their advertising, if only to be able to treat them with the tone of indulgent if world-weary amusement that befits the truly great bluffer. One such emporium informs that 'le hard sans limites – ça existe', and then, in smaller letters, 'à St. Lazare'. Another establishment, on the **rue des Ecoles** advertises live couples performing naked in nets over your head, which must be as uncomfortable for the couples as it is presumably damply unpleasant for the spectators. The proper attitude is to dismiss all these things, though for different reasons:

1. The **Moulin** and the **Folies** are pale shadows of their former glories
2. The newer clubs simply have nothing to do with anything genuinely French.

This line of nostalgia can usefully be pursued with the red-light districts as well, particularly that of **rue St. Denis**. What used to be a good, simple streetwalkers' street has been taken over by American bars and peep-shows; and regulars report the **filles** aren't what they used to be either. They certainly aren't what they used to be in the **Bois de Boulogne**. Here, along the avenues that criss-cross the woods, you can find just about every kind of bizarre trans-sexual in the book. Most of them are, for some impenetrable reason, Brazilian. The whole thing is highly organised at night and the entire **bois** divided into sections, depending on the preferences and merchandise of its occupants. All human life is there in its infinite variety, and it's surpising how varied it can be.

Like any major city, Paris has a flourishing gay scene, which you can easily become involved in if you aren't careful. Among the peep-shows and porn cinemas of St. Denis and Pigalle you will find **films gays**, and there are a large number of gay and lesbian bars which don't seem to object to the presence of the occasional straight. The Paris gay scene is both less aggressive and less defensive than its London counterpart, and there is at least one gay bar in the Marais where you can still get a beer for seven francs until two in the morning, if you don't mind having your buttocks cruised by gentlemen in boxer shorts. Incidentally, the French for AIDS is **SIDA (Syndrome immuno-défaillante acquise**). It is also a good idea to be familiar with the following:

Putain – (1) (Excl.) Oh dear!; (2) (n.f.) lady of doubtful morals

Pute – as **putain** (2), above.

Maquereau – (1) mackerel: (2) gentlemen who makes a living out of promoting the interests of **putain** (2).

Micheton – gentleman who avails himself of the services of **putain** (2).

Merde! – (Excl.) Oh dear! (N.B. can be combined with **putain** (1) to create a more powerful expostulation: thus "**putain de merde!**" or "**putain de putain de merde!**"; or even "**putain de putain de putain de putain de merde!**")

Pouffiasse – young lady of rather easy virtue (e.g. "**Toutes les Anglaises sont des pouffiasses**")

Un salaud – an unpleasant person

Une salope – (1) an unpleasant person (f.); (2) a lady of lax habits

Salopard – **salaud**, but stronger.

Pédé – gentleman of doubtful sexual orientation

Costaud – large gentleman

Armoire – (1) (Lit.) a wardrobe; (2) (Fig.) **costaud**

The Police

Don't be misled by their charmingly traditional air: although the French police still wear **képis**, the silly peaked hats, they are not to be trifled with, having an enduring reputation for public obstructiveness and private brutality. This was briefly checked by the Socialist government of the early 'eighties, but since the election in March 1986 of a right-wing government, on a law-and-order platform, they have returned to their old habits with a vengeance, and go about their business of harassing young people and racial minorities with renewed vigour. All this is greatly approved of in the **Seizième** where anyone who earns less than half a million francs is considered probably to be a criminal unless they can furnish constructive proof to the contrary.

But the ordinary **gendarme** (or **flic**, as you should get into the habit of calling them) is a paragon of mildness and respect for human rights when compared with the **CRS**. The CRS are the riot police: the initials are supposed to stand for **Compagnies Républic-aines de la Sécurité**: but, as every Parisian knows, this is an official fiction: in fact the letters indicate that you are dealing with '**Cons Racistes et Salauds**' (see Glossary for help with this). They are of a bestiality almost unparalleled among the security forces of the Western world, and are only let out on special occasions to baton-charge peaceful demonstrators in the Place de la Nation, to tear-gas student sit-ins in La Sorbonne, or to water-cannon visiting groups of old-age pensioners from Dijon. They are carried from place to place in armoured buses with metal grilles on the windows: the naive may imagine these grilles are to prevent bricks and other missiles from getting in: in

33

fact, as everyone realises sooner or later, they are to prevent the CRS from getting out.

French Lavatories

Sooner or later, and generally sooner, one has to make the acquaintance of these legendary facilities. One of the few myths about the French that is almost completely true is that they are unable to carry out the simplest plumbing. Even in the smartest modern apartments in the Seizième, one is quite likely, on turning on a tap in the wash-basin, to discover water bubbling up through the bath-plug. But it is with the lavatory (the idiomatic French for lavatory is **les chiottes**) that the French really excel, managing to combine the minimum of hygiene with the maximum of discomfort. For many years, perhaps centuries, in France 'flush toilet' meant that it was flush with the floor. In what might be a sign of uncharacteristic embarrassment, the French invariably refer to these mediaeval devices as **'toilettes turques'**, as if by blaming the Turks for it, they escape censure themselves. These still exist, usually in the darkest nether regions of the **louche**-er type of bar, generally next to a stained, vandalised, graffiti-ridden phone booth which only accepts pre-War currency. The toilette turque, generally one for both sexes, lurks malodorously behind a thin, wooden door with a broken lock and no light. This means that the unfortunate user has to squat in fetid darkness, trying to hold the door shut and at the same time avoid overbalancing into the rancid void. It is usually only when it is already too late that you discover that there isn't any paper there either. The greatest drawback of the toilette turque is

34

that it's impossible to read on one, unless you have impeccable balance, a pocket flash-light, and a taste for living dangerously.

But the toilette turque, or 'crouching crapper', as it has been known with a mixture of horror and ghastly fascination to generations of British tourists, is slowly becoming a thing of the past.

Another legendary feature of Parisian 'sanitary' arrangements, now sadly entirely vanished, was the **pissoir**. This as its name graphically suggests, was a urinal found on street corners, and constructed from iron lattice-work in such a way that almost every part of the body, except for that bit actually being employed at the time, was visible to passers-by. It was generally considered that the pissoirs, or **Vespasiens**, as they were known (presumably because they dated from the reign of the Roman emperor Vespasian), lent a whiff of raffish charm to the Parisian street scene, though that of course wasn't the only thing they lent a whiff of. Now entirely vanished (the last one, in the Place de la Victoire, disappeared a couple of years ago), the pissoirs have been replaced by a sort of high-tech unisex modular evacuation system, which stand in the main streets and squares. They are extremely conspicuous, and people go to extraordinary lengths to try to conceal the fact that they are about to avail themselves of these facilities. Inside, they are powerfully disinfected, highly sanitary, and very un-French. Every fifteen minutes or so, the interior is completely hosed down with terrifying force and suddenness, presumably to discourage their use for any other purposes. They can be dangerous: a little girl suffocated in one a couple of years ago. All in all, the safest thing to do in Paris (if you can manage it) is not to go to the lavatory at all.

Doctors

One of the most interesting and reliable indices of cultural variance (apart from the lavatory) is the medical profession. Broadly speaking there are in France two types of doctor:

1. The first is the elderly, old-fashioned family practitioner with a dingy surgery in Montparnasse who is liable to harass you sexually if you are a woman (and, in exceptional circumstances, if you are a man as well): he always has plenty of time to talk to you and discuss your (and sometimes his) most intimate problems; the only thing he won't do is cure you.

2. The second type is young, brisk, white-coated, ultra-efficient, and more often than not a woman. She will give you at least thirty seconds of her time, before whisking you out of her office with a prescription for a placebo of one sort or another. She won't cure you either.

It is also worth knowing that the French are inclined to attribute almost any malady to the state of their livers. In Britain if you visit a doctor, they are likely to tell you you have a virus or an allergy, and give you antibiotics. In France, they will tell you that you have something wrong with your liver, and give you a suppository. The French for liver trouble is **crise de foie**, not to be confused with **une crise de la foi**, which is a crisis of faith.

Beaux Arts

The supermarket of French Arts is the Centre Georges Pompidou in the Place Beaubourg, or **Le Beaubourg** as everyone calls it. (The French hate calling things after dead statesmen and will go to almost any lengths to avoid it, as you must if you are to be taken seriously as a connoisseur of Paris.)

The building itself, hailed by some as a masterpiece of modern design, looks like a five-storey oil-refinery, and was accurately described by its architect as 'A building built inside out', as all the pipes, ducts, escalators, etc., are on the outside. Opinions are sharply divided as to its architectural merits: **'C'est une immense merde'***, said one evidently satisfied taxpayer shortly after it opened in 1977, but the general view now, at least among the younger Parisians, is favourable.

Whatever you might think of it architecturally, its permanent collection of modern art is among the best in the world (say this as though you've seen all the others), it mounts highly imaginative special exhibitions and it has a very good library. You should find out what special exhibitions are on at the time, in order to appear knowledgeable (no need actually to *go* to any of them – they are rather expensive), and it is advisable to be informed about some which have taken place in the past, to give the impression that your knowledge has some depth to it. In 1982, for instance, the basement well was occupied by 384 television sets, programmed on video to broadcast patterns of images, arranged such that the overall effect was of three bands of colour, reds, monchromes and blues. The creation of a Japanese artist working in Paris, it was called *Tricolore Vidéo*. More recently, the Beaubourg mounted an exhibition, if that's the right word, conceived and put together by a group of writers, philosophers, artists, linguists, and general-purpose intel-

*It's a huge pile of shit.

lectuals (in whom Paris abounds), called *Les Immatér-iaux*, and which featured video, concrete sculpture, light effects, computer-interaction (among other things); visitors had to wear radio headpones, which picked up a variety of signals depending on where you were, ranging from bizarre noises to theoretical manifestos and a short story by Borges. It is important to have very powerful opinions about such matters: it doesn't matter whether you're in favour or not.

Still among the avant-garde, it is worth remembering that there is a Museum of Holography opposite the Beaubourg – and don't forget the exploits of the great Bulgarian artist and raving loony **Christo**, who wrapped the **Pont Neuf** in a coating of yellow plastic in 1985.

For more conventional types of art, there's always the **Louvre**. It is always full of tourists: try saying "It's usually less crowded in February". You could try the old art-students' trick of trying to race between its three great masterpieces, the *Venus de Milo*, the *Samothrace* and the *Mona Lisa* in less than a minute. This requires planning, is not easy, and tends to attract the disapproval of everyone else in the place (which is of course a good reason for doing it).

At the end of the **Tuileries** is the Jeu de Paume, (literally squash court) which used to be the home of the great **Impressionists**. The collection has moved across the river to a new home in the **Musée d'Orsay**. You might try venturing the view that it's overrated: it is certainly overcrowded.

Facing the vast tarmac wasteland that is the **Place de la Concorde** (not named after the aircraft of the same name, though it is at least as noisy), are the **Grand Palais** and the **Petit Palais**, iron and glass structures of a nineteenth-century vintage, and of a type until recently thought hideous, but now much admired. These put on special exhibitions (**expos**: always call them this), and it is worth knowing what's on there, either from the advertisements in the Métro (the only ones that, unlike almost all other French poster advertising, do not feature naked female breasts), or by buying one of the two small weekly guides to what's on, *Pariscope*, (The *Time Out* of Paris) or *L'Officiel des Spectacles*. These are indispensable for those who want (as all bluffers do) to appear **branché** (see Glossary). These are, unlike any guide-books except an extremely old and battered Baedeker, acceptable to be seen with (Parisians buy them too). They also make for amusing reading in the **spectacles érotiques** section (see Sex).

Acquaintance with the new **Picasso** Museum is probably essential. The French had the good sense to extract his enormous death-duties in the form of pictures, Picasso's own Picassos – the ones he would not part with. It only opened recently, in the **Hôtel Salé**, so-called because it was built on the proceeds of a fortune made in salt, and is a masterpiece of modern museum design.

The most important thing is to gain a knowledge of the lesser-known galleries, and of the lesser-known things in the better-known galleries. Useful in this regard is the house of **Gustave Moraux**, fantastical painter and illustrator, which is in the **Dixième** near Trinité, and **Camille Claudel** who is worth mentioning, partly because she is currently trendy, and partly because she led an appallingly repressed and unrewarded life, and as such is excellent material for a devastating feminist critique of art as patriarchy (or something).

Theatre

The great French theatre **Comédie Française**, despite its name, tends to put on productions of unremitting seriousness. Generally, it is not a good idea to claim to have seen anything there, unless you revel in classical productions of classical drama, serious, highbrow, and filled largely with schoolchildren preparing for their **baccalauréat** (known universally as the 'Bac'). The French are even more earnest about their classical theatre than the British are about Shakespeare. Better ground is the more experimental end of the business, and a good name to drop is that of **Ariane Mnouchkine**, whose extraordinary interpretations (notably of Shakespeare in the form of Japanese Noh drama) have won her a great reputation. Don't bother about whether or not it is deserved.

The **Atélier** has put on some influential shows in recent years, including a version of Diderot's philosophical dialogue *Le Neveu de Rameau*, an adaptation of Queneau's *Exercices de Style* (God knows how), and a revival of Becket's *En Attendant Godot* (a good idea to refer to it in French). It is also worth noting that **La Huchette** has been showing Ionesco's *La Cantatrice Chauve* continuously since 1957, and it's a sight better than *The Mousetrap*.

Cinema

Paris cinemas are plentiful, cheaper than their London counterparts (particularly on Mondays), and tend to get most films well before we do. The relevant pages of *Pariscope* or *L'Officiel* are invaluable, but you have to crack the complex code that is their classification system. The more reputable cinemas often specialise in major retrospectives of the work of important directors: Hitchcock and Lubitsch, for some reason, seem perennially popular. The confident bluffer will insist on going to see either a French language film, or a film subtitled in French, and must practise making the appropriate vocal reactions at the proper moments. It's no good simply following the example of those around you: you have to initiate. A kind of ironic, clipped laugh is the best for general use, as it conveys the impression that you've observed a particularly clever and subtle concealed joke which is beyond the comprehension of most of the audience. It is important to know that the letters 'v.o.' in the film listings stand for **version originale**, i.e. subtitled and undubbed; the dubbed films are marked 'v.f.' (**version française**) and are to be avoided at all costs.

The Paris of the fifties, slightly decrepit, down-at-heel, but still vital and exuberant, was the stuff of films made by directors like **Jacques Becker**: confident essays in **film noir**, concentrating on an underworld largely peopled by **Jean Gabin**. In the sixties and seventies this population was widened to include **Belmondo** and **Delon**. The most successful recent **policier** was perhaps *La Balance*, notable for its stark realism, and the fact that it didn't star either Belmondo or Delon (but rather the delectable **Nathalie Baye**). Of the **nouvelle vague** directors of the sixties, **Godard** is perhaps most closely associated with Paris. His early films borrowed many of the elements of the thrillers that had gone before, including seedy **milieux** and improbably attractive stars.

The most recent development has been the emergence of a kind of self-conscious preening **chic**, as manifested by films like **Beineix's** *Diva* and **Besson's**

Subway. These works of young style-conscious directors are by no means representative of the mainstream (which is still dominated by the **policier**, Belmondo and Delon, to an extent unimagined by people who don't know the place, and tend to think of French films as involving deep intellectualism and elegant adultery).

Music

Contemporary French music consists of:

1. Extremely serious minded singer-songwriters (**auteur-compositeur-chanteur** is how you should refer to them) with pretensions to the status of poets.
2. Quite appalling bland pop sung by identikit **chanteuses**, almost exclusively concerned with **l'amour**.

There are exceptions but a good line, particularly for the older bluffer, is to claim that the French song died with **Edith Piaf**.

Anyone wanting to pretend to a knowledge of what life is like for the ordinary yob-in-the-street in the **Banlieue** must listen to the music of **Renaud**. Briefly notorious in Britain for his brilliant and irreverent song about Mrs. Thatcher, he is in France, and particularly in Paris, a cult-hero with a huge following. He is a leather-jacketed, long-haired figure; a guitarist and songwriter of some distinction, chronicling urban decay and alienation. An anarchist by temperament, he pokes fun at the pretensions of bourgeois life – he is the scourge of the BCBG – and the iniquities of the social and political systems. He is ideal material for the bluffer in that he provokes extremely strong reactions, ranging from a deep loathing to a kind of idolatry. His songs are particularly valuable as they are written in a French so richly argotic that many French people can't understand them. Thus you can always invent your way out of having to explain their meanings.

Another figure remarkable for his ability to **épater le Bourgeois**, is **Serge Gainsbourg**. Famous for living with **Jane Birkin** (whom for some reason the French find extremely sexy) he was the author of *Je t'Aime*, a song famous for having been banned for its heavy breathing. He's still going strong, and scandalising millions. For example he caused a furore by burning a 500 franc note on a television chat-show to demonstrate how rich he is. It is an interesting index of the French character, that this caused a far greater public reaction than any of his increasingly erotic songs seem to have done.

Literature

Two things are important here: the first is the **nouveau roman**, or new novel, a form pioneered in the sixties by people like **Robbe-Grillet**, **Simon** and **Sollers**. The **nouveau roman** is a self-consciously experimental form which does away with outmoded things like plot and character.

The second thing to be aware of is the current significance of 'structuralism' and 'post-structuralism'. The state of the former can be determined by the fact that nobody now claims to be one. As for the latter, the term covers just about everything. A name to conjure with in this regard is **Julia Kristeva**, a psychoanalytic critic of Bulgarian origin and impenetrable obscurity, who happens to be married to Sollers.

Politics

Ever since the French revolution, and no doubt before
it as well, the Parisians have been obsessed with politics. It is, along with cheese, one of the two ubiquitous
topics of French conversation. It is advisable for you
to be aware of this, and of some of the salient features
of French political life, and of its major figures.

France is currently in its **Fifth Republic**, established by de Gaulle in 1958, after what amounted to a
military coup to overthrow the **Fourth Republic**, a
ramshackle regime of rapidly-falling administrations
that had 'governed' France since the Second World
War. The Fifth Republic was set up with two very
clear goals in mind: to restore political stability, and
to keep de Gaulle in power more or less for life.

In this it largely succeeded but it is patently
unsuited to doing anything else, as the current govern-
mental situation demonstrates. Essentially, there is
a directly elected President, and a Parliament. The
President is elected for seven years, the Parliament
for five, and this means that at any particular time it
is quite possible for the President to be of one political
persuasion and the Parliament of another. This makes
for a fair amount of confusion, and the resulting mess,
which the French colourfully call **cohabitation**, is
certainly less than a happy marriage.

There are four major political parties: the Communists, the Socialists, the UDF and the RPR. The
Communists have been losing ground steadily for
twenty years, and their influence is restricted principally to older voters in the Banlieue, the so called 'Red

Belt'. By contrast, the **Socialists** have been going from strength to strength. Since the party was invented by **Mitterrand** in 1970 to help make him President, it has steadily increased its support, princiapally at the expense of the Communists. The **UDF** (**Union Démocratique Française**) was created by another individual, **Giscard d'Estaing**, in order for him to become President. This more or less free-lance invention of political parties is a feature of the Fifth Republic, started of course by de Gaulle and his Gaullists: no-one was ever quite sure what they stood for, apart from de Gaulle (and if you can stand for de Gaulle, you can stand for anything). The successor to the Gaullist party (which actually outlived de Gaulle by a few years, rather like a headless body) is the **RPR** (**Rassemblement pour la République**) a conservative grouping of power-hungry individuals, principal and most nakedly ambitious of whom is **Jacques Chirac**, the major adversary of Mitterrand.

There are three major qualifications you need in order to be President of France, apart from personal ambition, and the ability to invent a party. These are: a regal bearing, a balding head, and an enormous nose.

The last is perhaps the most essential. It is his lack of this qualification which in many people's eyes disqualifies Chirac from the position he so obviously covets. De Gaulle (who, according to Churchill 'looked like a female llama, surprised in her bath') possessed all three in abundance and it was only when his regal bearing took a battering at the hands of the students in May '68 that he eventually had to step down. Giscard rather overdid the regal bearing, and was a bit short on the nose, but has a perfect bald crown to compensate: Mitterrand scores heavily on the nose.

History of Paris

Paris has a long and wonderful history, unwinding rather slowly, at the rate of about three revolutions a century.

Origins

When all Gaul was divided into three parts, there was a tribe in the North Eastern part called the **Parisii**, and it is from them that Paris gets its name. Not much is known about them, except that they lacked a great deal of the urbane sophistication of later Parisians such as Yves Montand, and were more devoted to rock throwing than fine arts or haute cuisine. They were, therefore, the forerunners of the Paris Mob, a group much maligned in fiction and history books. The Romans took a fancy to the ambiance of Paris and settled on what is now the **Ile de la Cité**, but, with the Decline and Fall of the Roman Empire, Paris, like the rest of Europe, entered a period of political instability marked by waves of invasions. The most threatening was that of Attila the Hun in 451 A.D. He and his hordes reached Paris, but the city was saved by a young woman named **Geneviève**, who inspired the defenders of the city to an unusual level of heroic unity. Attila was repelled (militarily speaking) and Sainte Geneviève has since been the patron saint of Paris.

It wasn't long before those claiming to be kings of France made Paris their capital. The first to do so was **Clovis**, who sounds sweet and cuddly, but who was a fiercely ambitious man, fancying himself as Holy Roman Emperor. Ambition has been the downfall of every French king except **Saint Louis**, the one who had the Blues. Another trend started by Clovis was the tendency to see the history of Paris as the history of the whole of France. Only **Marshal Pétain** has gone against this, when he moved to Vichy in 1940, and look what happened to him.

Suffice it to say that by the year 622, Paris already had the reputation of being a den of iniquity. This attracted the then king, **Dagobert**, who moved into Paris and, says a contemporary account, 'surrendered himself to limitless debauchery'. Plus ça change, as they say.

Medieval Paris

By the year 1000, Paris, under King **Hugh Capet** (the French have maintained surnames for some of their kings, as though one Frenchman might turn to another and say: 'oh, *that* Hugh Capet. . . .'), had become a handsome as well as debauched city. The University of Paris was founded and work begun on **Notre Dame**. By the outbreak of the Hundred Years War (which actually lasted 115 years, the extra fifteen years being added as service wasn't included), Paris, with 150,000 inhabitants, could claim the cultural hegemony of Europe – not much of a claim, really, when you consider what was going on in the rest of the Continent.

Cultural it may have been, but Paris played a decidedly inactive part in the Hundred Years War. There wasn't a battle there. The Kings of France refused to recruit troops there (rulers of France have always feared arming the citizens of Paris). **Joan of Arc** didn't capture it. The garrison refused to co-operate with anybody.

So the only other memorable happenings in Medieval Paris were the completion of Notre Dame, the building of lots of slums and monasteries, and the Saint

Bartholomew's Day Massacre. This took place on 24th
August, 1572, and was the first great 'set-piece' spec-
tacular of violence in the history of Paris. It started with
bells ringing and one or two stabs at assassination
but rapidly deteriorated into an appalling massacre
of Protestant Huguenots by Catholics under the supervision of **Catherine de Medici**, famous throughout
Europe for her cabinet of poisons, her trafficking in the
Black Arts and her sexually-deviant sons. She is also
famous in French history as the first ruler to have a
hated minister. Since Catherine's time, every ruler of
France has had at least one hated minister.

Louis XIV: The Sun King
Louis XIV had two hated ministers, the Cardinals
Richelieu and **Mazarin**. Parisians mostly remember
him as the man who moved his court and palace out of
the city to **Versailles**, where the atmosphere was said
to be healthier. This made it very inconvenient for later
revolutionaries, who had to traipse all the way out to
Versailles to get hold of kings and queens and bring
them back to Paris to have their heads lopped off.

The French Revolution
THE French Revolution is the one of 1789, which had
a stream of violent set pieces: The Tennis Court Oath,
the Fall of the Bastille, the March of the Women of
Paris to Versailles (to bring the King back), the
September Massacres of 1792, the Execution of Louis
XVI in the **Place de la Concorde**, the Death of
Marat, the Executions of **Marie Antionette, Char-
lotte Corday, Danton, Robespierre** and several
hundred more, and the Clearing of the Streets of Paris
in October 1794 by the young **Napoleon Bonaparte**
and his Whiff of Grapeshot.

Bits of the Revolution did take place outside Paris, but not many. Even the Marseillais brought 'La Marseillaise' to Paris to make it famous.

What is worth noting, is that, despite the ceaseless activity of Madame **La Guillotine** (invented as a humane killer), Paris kept its head during those awful years. The Annual Art Exhibition was held every year at the Paris Salon, and those artists who were executed died (sadly) for their politics rather than their art, bad though much of it was. When **Louis XVI** was a prisoner in the Temple, awaiting his trial and death, he had three cooks, a scullion, a turnspit, a steward and assistant, a boy, a keeper of the plate and three waiters. His dinner menu included three soups, four entrees, two roasts, four or five side dishes, fruits, cheeses, Champagne and at least five other wines. All this when many in the city were starving. Similarly, when in prison, **Madame du Barry** managed three changes of costume a day. There is a sense of 'style' about the worst excesses of the French Revolution that should have pleased even Lady Bracknell.

Napoleon Bonaparte

Although a Corsican who spent most of his life racing round Europe fighting battles, Napoleon is closely linked to Paris. Some say he was the first to give cohesion to the Parisian style – the beginnings of French kitsch that is rampant today in so much of its 'objets' and 'meubles'. Like so many of his type, Napoleon was really a failed actor, more a histrionic figure than an historical one, more at home at the **Comédie-Française** than the **Ecole Militaire**, with **Grand Guignol** than the **Grand Armée**. This explains such memorable scenes in his life as his self crowning at his Coronation, baring his breast to those sent to arrest

him and begging them to shoot, numerous tearful fare-
wells at **Fontainebleu** and elsewhere (to his wife, to
his mistress, to his troops, to France), and the constant
apoplectic haranguing of Imperial guardsmen twice
his size. Only an actor can behave like that.

On his way to St. Helena, Napoleon left Paris the
Bourse, Les Invallides, the **Madeleine**, the **Column
of Vendôme** (subsequently moved), the **Arc de
Triomphe**, massive debts, dreadful slums (people were
sleeping thirty to a room), and a shortage of men in
their active years.

The Revolution of 1830
This was a totally Parisian affair and quite implau-
sibly romantic. Indeed, some see it as primarily the
work of **Victor Hugo, Berlioz, Madame de Staël** and
Delacroix. In three glorious days during July, 1830,
Charles X, the last of the Bourbons, was driven from
Paris (to the strains of La Marseillaise – as effective
then as it was in *Casablanca*), the **Hôtel de Ville** was
stormed, and a citizen king, **Louis Philippe**, was elected.

The Revolution of 1848
Only the French could 'elect' a 'citizen king', and such
an obviously whimsical notion clearly couldn't last. To
speed his departure, Louis Philippe appointed a hated
minister named **Guizot**, who rashly banned a political
banquet although he must have had some idea how
important food is to the average Parisian. The crowd
rose. Barricades were thrown up. The Hôtel de Ville
was stormed. Louis Philippe fled across the Channel
to Esher, by way of Newhaven. Not long after reaching
Esher, Louis Philippe very understandably died.

Some see the Revolution of 1848 as the product of
Dumas, Balzac and **George Sand**.

A Bonapartist Interlude
At this point Paris was rebuilt under the supervision of **Georges Haussman**, Prefect of the Seine. Much of today's Paris is the result of his work, where whole sections of the city were destroyed to make way for offices, department stores, exhibition halls, and boulevardes wide enough to permit cavalry to charge down them, and too wide for barricades to be easily thrown across them. Haussman's Paris has been described as 'needless monotony only partly relieved by the planting of trees', a nicely dismissive phrase.

The other great achievements of **Napoleon III** were the pioneering of sidewalk cafés, the **Can-Can**, the **Folies Bergères** and the first **Paris Exhibition** of 1855. There have been Paris Exhibitions ever since, gradually degenerating to the level where they devote themselves to awarding medals for ice creams.

Franco Prussian War: The Siege of Paris
After the awful defeat of the French army at the battle of Sedan in 1870, Napoleon III fled across the Channel to Chislehurst, which must have been even worse than Esher, and led to his almost immediate death. The Hôtel de Ville was stormed, and the Third Republic was proclaimed.

The Prussian army surrounded Paris, and a five month siege began, the only person managing to escape being the Minister of the Interior, **Léon Gambetta**, who departed by balloon after joining other wealthy bourgeois in eating one of the elephants from the Paris zoo, other food being in short supply.

The Commune
There followed a very complicated period of Parisian history. Basically, the city tore itself in two. Right

fought Left, making it even easier for the Prussians to enter the city and have William II proclaimed Emperor of Germany in the Hall of Mirrors at Versailles. The Left saw themselves betrayed by the Right, and hundreds of thousands of 'classes dangereuses' and 'impatientes' simmered with anger. This time the hated minister was **Thiers**, who fled to Versailles and made several dishonourable deals with the Prussians, whereby French POWs were released to go back and fight the Communes, established by the Left in Paris.

The thing to remember about the **Communards** is that, whatever Marx has said, they weren't really Communists. All they wanted was the right to organize their own city (taxes, budgets, police courts, public services, etc.) and abolish pawnbrokers and night work in the bakeries. They made no attacks on property, and the Bank of France calmly financed both the Commune and its enemies at the same time.

For their pains, the Communards were blown to pieces by the troops of Thiers: twenty thousand Parisian men, women and children being shot, and a further thirteen thousand deported. The final battle took place in the **Faubourg St. Antoine**, still a place of pilgrimage for the Left, who go to the far wall of the Cemetery **Père Lachaise** where some 200 Communards died literally with their backs to the wall – le mure des fédérés.

The Hôtel de Ville was not only stormed, but destroyed.

La Belle Epoque
This is the name given to the Good Old Days, the period from roughly 1889 (the year in which the Eiffel Tower was built) to 1914. For those 25 years Paris was 'the' place to be: a place where you could have a night

out with an eight course meal, a visit to the Opera, and a woman of your choice, and still get change from three sous.

In La Belle Epoque Paris had **Monet, Sisley, Berthe Morisot, Degas, Toulouse-Lautrec, Ravel, Debussy, Sarah Bernhardt, Baudelaire, Verlaine, Renoir**, the **Lumière Brothers**, the three Louis (**Blériot, Renault** and **Chevrolet**) and the first Métro line.

World War I

Since there wasn't a Hôtel de Ville to storm any more, Paris remained surprisingly quiet during the First World War. The main events were a shortage of taxis in 1914 (when they were used to transport the French Army to the Marne, only forty miles away) and again in 1918 (when the German advance to within shelling distance of Paris forced many of the richer inhabitants to take taxis in the opposite direction).

The Paris Riots of 1934

Although they evolved from a classic confrontation between Right and Left, the Paris Riots of 1934 were sparked off when **Edouard Daladier** fired the head of the Comédie-Française, ostensibly for producing Shakespeare's undemocratic *Coriolanus*, and replaced him with the Chief of the Sûreté. It was a very French affair, with the usual complication of a highly artistic involvement. Daladier then cast himself in the role of hated minister, loathed by Left and Right alike. A vast crowd gathered in the **Place de la Concorde**, which, bearing in mind the number of times it has seen civil violence in the history of Paris, might have been more aptly named 'Place de la Discorde'. Stones were thrown. Shots were fired. Barricades were thrown up.

A pitched battle took place in which the Police sided with the Right and the Government was overthrown.

World War II

The Third Republic staggered on for another six years, to be destroyed when the victorious German armies marched into the **Place de l'Etoile** in 1940, thus beginning the Occupation. The Germans stayed in Paris this time, and **Pétain** shuffled off to Vichy and dishonour. One of the first laws the German army imposed after occupying Paris, was that Parisians should cross roads only at appointed places, which tells you an awful lot about Parisians and the German army.

The history of Paris in the Second World War is memorable for two things: Ingrid Bergman's failure to meet Humphrey Bogart in time to catch the train at the **Gare de Lyon**, and the Libération.

The Libération was begun by the citizens of Paris in late August 1944. Three thousand of them died, and you can still see plaques spread around the city marking many of the places where they were killed. Hitler ordered the German commander, General von Choltitz, to destroy the city, but the General refused, and Paris was saved from ruin until the Tour Montparnasse was built some twenty years later.

One of the most famous photographs of Paris is that of **Charles de Gaulle** marching along the Champs Elysées the day after the Libération (**General Leclerc** unforgivably got there one day ahead of him) with crowds of Parisians pouring along behind him. The Fourth Republic was born.

54

Death of the Fourth Republic

The Fourth Republic was fourteen years old when it died of Algérie Française. Nobody was stoned in Paris. The Fifth Republic was born.

Revolution of 1968

Only Paris could have staged a revolution of University students and lecturers that all but brought down the Republic. It is hard to imagine a similar thing taking place in Oxford, or even London. Students fought a pitched battle in the Latin Quarter with the **CRS**. Paving stones were hurled. Tear gas fired. The barricades went up. Half a million students and workers marched across Paris and occupied the **Odéon** Theatre, the **Opéra**, the **Opéra Comique** and the **Beaux Arts**, presumably in Paris's age old belief that he who controls the arts, controls Paris. Where the insurgents of other nations would make for the Post Office, the Telephone Exchange, the Broadcasting Centre and the printing presses, Parisians go for cinemas and dance halls. Only after de Gaulle made a dreadful appearance on TV did the demonstrators attack the **Bourse**, police stations and other strongholds of capitalism.

De Gaulle flew away to meet military leaders in eastern France and Germany. He returned, clearly feeling a lot better, and made a second, better TV appearance. This greatly encouraged the Gaullists, who poured down the **Champs Elysées** in support. (People always 'pour' down or along the Champs Elysées – it may be the only way to avoid being run over). The Fifth Republic was saved.

The rest is history.

GLOSSARY OF IDIOMATIC FRENCH

The successful bluffer must have a fluent command of just enough French to give other people the impression that he or she has a fluent command of French. This turns out in fact to be surprisingly little. You will already have gleaned some of the vital terms from the text, but we append here a short glossary of others which the ambitious will wish to have at their fingertips. In bluffing, a little learning goes a long way, and is an essential rather than a dangerous thing.

Some Useful Nouns

mec – man

nana – young lady

supernana – extremely attractive young lady

gonzesse – young lady, generally in whom the speaker has a particular interest

connard – stupid person (m.)

connasse – stupid person (f.)

con – stupid person (indeterminate: see also Adjectives below)

petit con – a term of contempt

pauvre con – as above

pauvre mec – as above

copain, copine – friend (m. and f.)

petit copain, petite copine – boy-friend, girl-friend (these terms are hideously twee and should only be used ironically)

jules, julie – boyfriend, girlfriend, but more acceptable

pote – friend (on no account confuse with **pute**)

teigne – irritating person

voyou – hooligan

alcolo – someone given to the use of alcoholic beverages

clochard – tramp

intelo – (contemptuous) an intellectual

prolo – the working class

boulot – job (this is now slightly **démodé:** the proper French for 'job' is **le job**)

l'héxagone – France

les ros-bifs – the British (NB: entirely complimentary)

cageot – less than attractive older lady

branleur – (1) someone who practises sexual self-stimulation; (2) someone generally held in contempt

bagarre – dispute, generally of a violent nature

baston – **bagarre**

policier – a thriller, film or novel (**un roman-policier** is a crime novel); in trendy circles they are called **'polars'**

flic, poulte, laipou (see Verlan, below) – cop

la flicaille – the fuzz

bagnole – motor-car

moto, bécan, tomo (see Verlan, below)– motor-bicycle

The Family

le frangin – brother

la frangine – sister

la maternelle – mother

le paternel – father

la belle – sister-in-law

le beauf – brother-in-law

la belle-doche – mother-in-law

les gosses, les mômes – children

Parts of the Body

le bec – the mouth

le tif – the hair

le pif – the nose

les quilles – legs

les nichons, les miches, les roberts, les blagues-à-tabac, la gorge, les tétons, les ropolots – breasts

la bite, la queue, la quequette, le zob, le zeb, le zizi, l'anguille de caleçon – male member

le chat, la chatte, la praline, le zizi (as well) – female equivalent

le cul, les fesses, l'oignon, le panier à crottes – bottoms (m. and f.)

Adjectives

con – stupid

débile – con

baclé – a little run down

démodé – old fashioned

branché – having one's finger on the pulse

chébran – **branché** (see Verlan, below)

moche – bad

pourri – roughly **moche** (Verlan, **ripou**)

sympa – good, nice

minable – lamentable

lamentable – minable

louche – grotty

supersexy – (self-explanatory)

chaud – (1) hot; (2) in a state of sexual excitement (note the expressions **lapin chaud** and **chatte chaude** for people in this condition)

cool – good

supercool – very good

hypercool – extremely good

vachement chouette – really very good indeed

terrible – really very good (paradoxically)

Some Useful Phrases

tirer un coup – (Lit.) fire a shot; (Fam.) have intimate relations with

baiser – (Fam.) **tirer un coup** (2) (it is very important to get this right: it does *not* mean 'kiss' any more. 'To kiss' is **embrasser**; 'a kiss' is **un bisou**)

foutre – **baiser**, but it figures in a variety of idiomatic expressions, such as:

fous le camp – please go away

fous-moi la paix – please leave me alone

je m'en fous – I don't care

j'ai rien à foutre – I've got nothing to do

tu te fous de ma gueule – I don't think you're taking me seriously

qu'est-ce que tu fous là-bas, espèce de petit connard? – what do you think you're doing there, my man?

va te faire foutre – I'd prefer it if you left immediately

c'est de la foutaise – it's a load of crap

c'est un bordel! – it's a mess!

être en cloque – to be pregnant

avoir du monde au balcon – to be well-endowed in the bust

avoir un vélo dans la tête – to be in a state of some confusion

avoir des chauve-souris dans le dongeon – to be somewhat deranged (the French for 'mad' is **dingue**, or **dingo**)

être fauché – to be short of funds (N.B. **la balle**, the franc; **une brique**, 10,000 francs)

être à côté de ses pompes – to be mentally disturbed

avoir la dalle – to be extremely hungry

crever de la dalle – to be dying of hunger (N.B. **crever**, to die) but perhaps most importantly of all:

ché pas – I've no idea (contraction of '**je ne sais pas**')

ché pas, moi – as above, only more emphatic. This is perhaps the most commonly used phrase in French.

Verlan

This is the really subtle bit. If you want to create French slang, this is how you go about doing it (it only works for two-syllable words, unfortunately). You simply reverse the order of the syllables. Thus **le moto** becomes **le tomo; branché** becomes **chébran;** and it can be done with phrases as well, so **laisser tomber** (to let go, to drop someone, to let them down, to chuck them) becomes **laisser béton** (incidentally, the title of one of Renaud's early songs). The clever bluffer who knows some disyllabic words in French can simply make these up, secure in the knowledge that:

a)   no-one will realise they've been invented, and
b)   someone else has almost certainly done it before.

The word **verlan** is itself **verlan** for **l'envers**, the reverse. Cunning, isn't it?

Even more sophisticated (so much so that most French people don't understand it) is **Largonji**. This consists in removing the first consonant from a word, replacing it with the letter 'l', then putting the name of the original letter at the end of the word. Thus **lamedé** is **largonji** for **la dame**, woman; and of course, **largonji** is itself **largonji** for **le jargon**, slang. This technique is harder to fake than **verlan**, but less essential: merely knowing that it exists is devastating enough.

These two methods are similar in conception to cockney rhyming-slang: but they are different in that, far from being quaint or **passé**, they are the mark of the extremely trendy: in fact, of the truly **chébran**.

THE AUTHOR

Born in Africa in order to avoid playing cricket for Yorkshire, Jim Hankinson has always striven to project an image of classy, cosmopolitan cool, something not easy to do if you live in Bolton. A regular visitor to Paris for more than ten years, he has researched this book diligently and with application in double-beds throughout the city. A brilliant linguist (he can say "Give me a beer" in six languages) he is now able to pass as a Frenchman, though not, unfortunately, in France.

On the strength of his earlier work *Bluffer's Guide to Philosophy*, he got a job at the philosophy department of McGill University, Montreal, where he now lives and teaches, hoping no-one will discover that he knows almost nothing about the subject.

His other interests include beer and sex, unfortunately for the latter generally in that order.

THE BLUFFER'S GUIDES

Available now:

The Bluffer's Guide to Accountancy	£1.00
The Bluffer's Guide to Antiques	£1.00
The Bluffer's Guide to Class	£1.00
The Bluffer's Guide to Computers	£1.00
The Bluffer's Guide to Consultancy	£1.00
The Bluffer's Guide to Golf	£1.00
The Bluffer's Guide to Hollywood	£1.00
The Bluffer's Guide to Management	£1.00
The Bluffer's Guide to Music	£1.00
The Bluffer's Guide to Paris	£1.00
The Bluffer's Guide to Philosophy	£1.00
The Bluffer's Guide to Teaching	£1.00
The Bluffer's Guide to Theatre	£1.00

Coming, June 1987:

The Bluffer's Guide to Wine	£1.00
The Bluffer's Guide to Publishing	£1.00
The Bluffer's Guide to Sex	£1.00
The Bluffer's Guide to Television	£1.00

All these books are available at your local bookshop or newsagent, or can be ordered direct from the publisher. Just tick the titles you require and fill in the form below. Prices and availability subject to change without notice.

Ravette Limited, 3 Glenside Estate, Star Road, Partridge Green, Horsham, West Sussex RH13 8RA.

Please send a cheque or postal order, and allow the following for postage and packing. UK 25p for one book and 10p for each additional book ordered.

Name ....

Address ....

....

THE BLUFFER'S GUIDES

In preparation:

Advertising
Architecture
Astrology
Ballet
Bank Managers
Beliefs
Bluffing
The Body
Cinema
The Classics
Defence
Espionage
Feminism
Finance
Gambling
High Society
Journalism
Law
Literature
Marketing
Millionaires
Modern Art
Opera
Photography

Politics
Property
Psychiatry
Public Relations
Secret Societies
Selling
Ski-ing
Stocks & Shares
Travel
Wine
World Affairs

The Americans
The Australians
The British
The French
The Germans
The Japanese

Amsterdam
Berlin
Hong Kong
Moscow
New York